FAVORITE HORSE BREEDS

THOROUGHBRED HORSES

by Cari Meister

AMICUS | AMICUS INK

Amicus High Interest and Amicus Ink are published by Amicus
P.O. Box 227, Mankato, MN 56002
www.amicuspublishing.us

Library of Congress Cataloging-in-Publication Data
Names: Meister, Cari, author.
Title: Thoroughbred horses / by Cari Meister.
Description: Mankato, Minnesota : Amicus, [2019] | Series: Favorite horse breeds | Includes index.
Identifiers: LCCN 2017036881 (print) | LCCN 2017048298 (ebook) | ISBN 9781681515090 (pdf) | ISBN 9781681514277 (library bound) | ISBN 9781681523477 (pbk.)
Subjects: LCSH: Thoroughbred horse--Juvenile literature.
Classification: LCC SF293.T5 (ebook) | LCC SF293.T5 M47 2019 (print) | DDC 636.1/32--dc23
LC record available at https://lccn.loc.gov/2017036881

Photo Credits: Dimitar Todorov/Alamy Stock Photo cover; Golubenko Svetlana/123RF 2; Scott Serio/Eclipse Sportswire/Getty 5; RG Reeve/Getty 6; catnap72/Getty 8–9; Pariyawit Sukumpantanasarn/123RF 10; Abramova_Kseniya/iStock 12; skif/iStock 14–15; otsphoto/Shutterstock 17; Chad Clarke/Alamy 18–19; vm/Getty 20–21; olgaIT/iStock 22

Editor: Wendy Dieker
Designer: Veronica Scott
Photo Researcher: Holly Young

TABLE OF CONTENTS

IT'S RACE DAY!

It is race day. The horses are in the gate. They stomp. They snort. A bell rings. They are off! They run. They are fast! They are thoroughbreds.

4
3
2
1
8
7
6

6

ROYAL HISTORY

The thoroughbred **breed** was started in England in the late 1600s and early 1700s. King James I and King Charles I wanted the fastest horses. They helped make these fast racehorses.

BORN TO RUN

A thoroughbred has long legs. It has strong **hindquarters**. That makes it powerful and fast. This horse was born to run!

Did You Know?

A thoroughbred can run up to 45 miles (72 km) per hour!

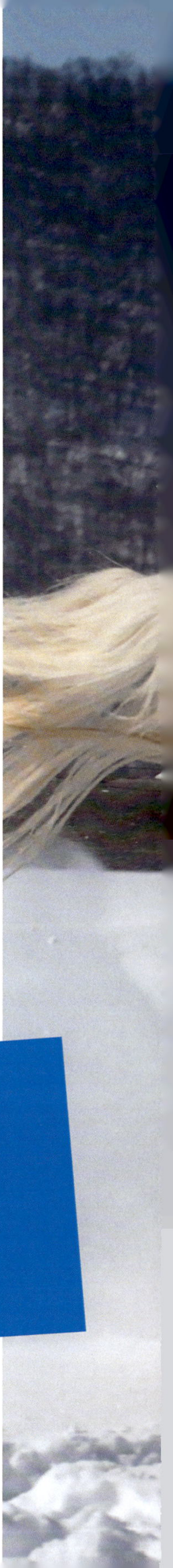

SPORTY HORSE

Thoroughbreds are alert and swift. They are good at many horse sports. They are good for playing **polo**. Some are jumping horses.

A STRONG RUNNER

Thoroughbreds have large hearts. A big heart can pump blood around the body better. It means the horse can run longer and faster.

Did You Know?

A thoroughbred's heart can weigh 22 pounds (10 kg)! Most horses' hearts are 14 pounds (6.3 kg).

SOLID COLORS

These horses come in many colors. Most are dark brown or **bay**. A white thoroughbred is rare. Most thoroughbreds are solid colors. Some have white marks.

LIVELY FOALS

A thoroughbred **foal** looks like its parents. It has a thin face, a short back, and a slim body. These foals are bold and lively.

HOT BLOODED

Thoroughbreds are called hot blooded. That means they can be hard to handle. They have a lot of spirit. They need a lot of training. A thoroughbred is not the best horse for a new rider.

A SLEEK HORSE

With the right training, this horse is smooth to ride. It is strong and able. It is sleek and athletic. It is fun to watch.

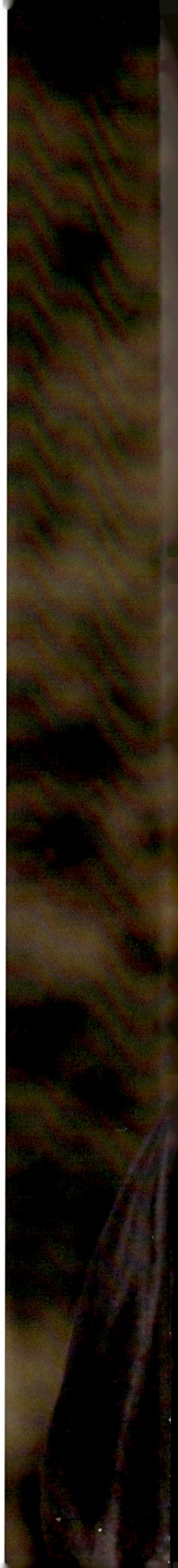

HOW DO YOU KNOW IT'S A THOROUGHBRED HORSE?

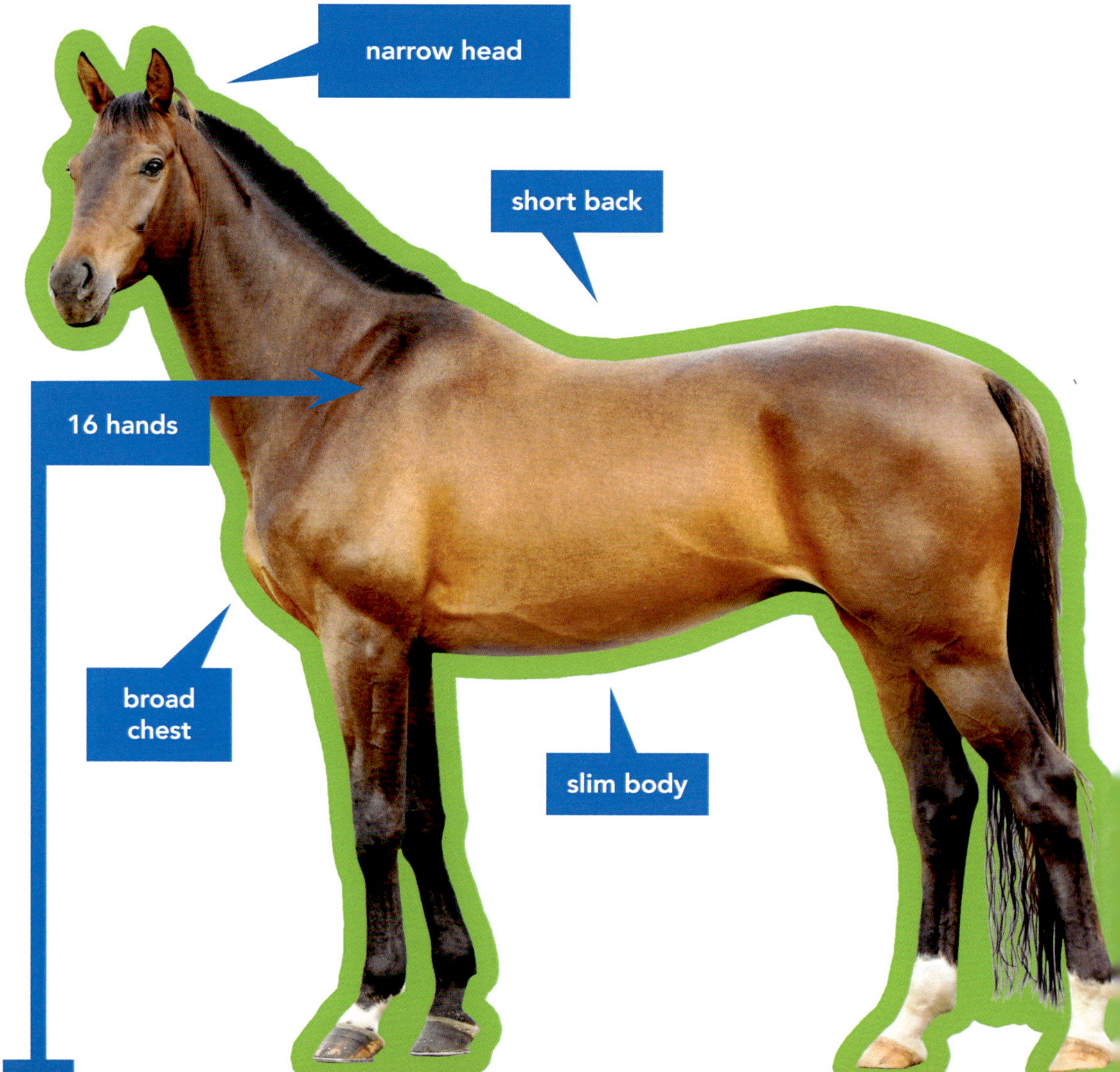

WORDS TO KNOW

bay – a horse color that is a dark reddish-brown coat with black mane and tail.

breed – a particular kind of horse that has certain features and characteristics and has ancestors of the same breed.

foal – a baby horse.

hindquarters – the back legs and rump of a horse.

polo – a game like field hockey played on horseback where players work in teams to hit a ball into a net.

LEARN MORE

Books

Hansen, Grace. *Thoroughbred Horses.* Minneapolis: Abdo Kids, 2017.

Young, Rae. *Drawing Thoroughbreds and Other Elegant Horses.* North Mankato, Minn.: Capstone Press, 2014.

Websites

17 Amazing Thoroughbred Horse Facts
https://www.karinabrez.com/blog/2016/10/25/17-amazing-thoroughbred-horse-facts

Blaze Magazine, For Horse Crazy Kids
www.blazekids.com

INDEX